D0723481

The Hazards

Sarah Holland-Batt was born in Southport, Queensland, in 1982 and has lived in Australia and the United States. She is the recipient of the WG Walker Memorial Fulbright Scholarship, Yaddo and MacDowell fellowships, and an Australia Council Literature Residency at the BR Whiting Studio in Rome, among other honours. Her first book, *Aria* (UQP, 2008), won a number of literary awards, including the Thomas Shapcott Poetry Prize, the artsACT Judith Wright Prize, and the FAW Anne Elder Award, and was shortlisted in the New South Wales Premier's Kenneth Slessor Prize and the Queensland Premier's Judith Wright Calanthe Award. She holds an MFA from New York University, and First Class Honours in Literature and an MPhil in English from the University of Queensland. She is presently a Senior Lecturer in Creative Writing at the Queensland University of Technology.

Sarah Holland-Batt
The Hazards

UQP

First published 2015 by University of Queensland Press
PO Box 6042, St Lucia, Queensland 4067 Australia

www.uqp.com.au
uqp@uqp.uq.edu.au

Cover design/illustration by Sandy Cull, gogoGingko
Author photograph by Anna Caldwell
Typeset in 11.5/14 pt Adobe Garamond by Post Pre-press Group, Brisbane
Printed in Australia by McPherson's Printing Group

Cataloguing-in-Publication data
is available at http://catalogue.nla.gov.au

ISBN 978 0 7022 5359 1 (pbk)
ISBN 978 0 7022 5515 1 (pdf)
ISBN 978 0 7022 5516 8 (epub)
ISBN 978 0 7022 5517 5 (kindle)

University of Queensland Press uses papers that are natural, renewable
and recyclable products made from wood grown in sustainable forests.
The logging and manufacturing processes conform to the environmental
regulations of the country of origin.

for Mavis K,
who taught me the names of things

Contents

Denn alles Fleisch, es ist wie Gras

I

Medusa

I have always loved the translucent life,
the concentricities
blooming around me
in a ripple-ring of nerves.
If I let my shadow cinch in,
whatever the soul is
billows out like hollow silk.
Needle by needle, I plume
into the rays of an underwater moon,
climbing pure and poisonous
in the drift of marine snow.
Nothing hangs quite so empty.
See how my mind skates,
vain and clear as melting ice.
It contracts with a heart's pulse:
selfish, selfish.
I glide savage, a stinging chandelier,
a brain trailing its nettles
through the anemone swell
and forests of stiff sea fir.
Malice swarms through me in a surge.
I know that flare, that bitter reason.
And I will float and flower
in my season.

This Landscape Before Me

Is unwritten, though it has lived in violence.

First the factory stood, quiet as an asylum.
Then the annihilating mallee with its red fists of blossoms
and the mountain ash creeping over it like a stain.

I have no proof, but I tell you
there were leadlight windows here once, barred.
They cast a little striped light on the women.

Now in scrub and yellow broom I stand on a history
braided and unbraided by stiff Irish wrists.
The rope and span and carded wool are unpicked
as are the faces and names.

Londonderry, Cork, Galway, Kildare –
as I say the words they are sucked away
to a hemisphere in darkness.

I will not presume to say
what suffering is or how it was meted out in this place.
At what point it breaks a body I cannot tell.

But this morning I saw a young rabbit
hunched in brush and shadow.
I saw its lesioned face, its legs too thin to scramble,
the blood-berry red and pink scab of its eye.

It had caught the disease
we brought here for it
and wanted a quiet place to die.

And it was lucky, or as lucky as it would get —
there was time and light, the hawks and dogs
had not been written yet, and were still out of sight.

The Orchid House

Pegged under banana trees
our backyard hothouse was fixed summer
that boiled all year, a green humpy
breathing gauze in meshy sheets.
Indoors it poured artificial rain.

Under that slatted sunlight
I crept the spider-heavy shelves
where exotics festered in their Latin names.
I torqued the twist-wires tight
around each trumpeting neck,
chivvied longlegs from potted dark
as outside the clouds blew back like years.

My grandfather spoke a strange pidgin there,
knew Cat's Face from Queen of Sheba,
Snake Flower, Soldier's Crest, Sulphur Tail.
A decade late, I found a wrinkled block of newsprint
under the orange crucifix,
six men waist-deep in the Mekong
where the war's end could never come.

Death never reached those suburbs, not really.
Bodies in their Sunday best
never lay on our kitchen table
stiff as celluloid dolls,
and last goodbyes
were told by nurses in chemical code.

When Grandad died, the wonky shack
grew wild, and creepers curtained over.
Through walls thin and threadbare
I heard them hissing, the cold wet tendrils
that could strangle, and grew on air:
teatree, tangle root, tongue.

Tropic Rain

Elephant ears like serving plates
stagger under it, tropic rain lashing sideways,
tripping like flapped tarp on tree palm,
lush, symphonic, no image in it. Embers sparked
from the water-forge hammer fern brim
and fling starwards into mango leaf.
Rain I have known like music, a tin oratorio
stammering like a frog into full throat
then overspilling to pinewood soakage,
crotchets quickened to a Cuban beat,
whipcrack on windowpane, slashing
down pawpaw skin, sledding in the green eaves.
Rain shuttering a suburb's eyelids,
rain in slant to louvre grain, sliced rain
with tinctures of iron in it, monsoon rain
so sheeted you stop at the verandah's brink
by a blurred world, all detail drummed,
tempered flat like the verge of sleep.
Then comes outpost rain, audible only
to insect ear, a trickle through weed thicket,
rain you might miss in an intermittent mizzle
like the stutter of magazine fire
that starts and stops and starts again.

Botany

After the rain, we went out in pairs
to hunt the caps that budded at night:
wet handfuls of waxtips and widows,
lawyer's wigs, a double-ringed yellow.

We shook them out onto gridded sheets,
the girls more careful than the boys,
pencilled notes on their size and shape,
then levelled a wood-press over their heads.

Overnight, they dropped scatter patterns
in dot-and-dash, spindles and asterisks
that stained the page with smoky rings,
blush and blot, coal-dust blooms.

In that slow black snow of spores
I saw a woodcut winter cart and horse
careen off course, the dull crash
of iron and ash, wheels unravelling.

All day, a smell of loam hung overhead.
We bent like clairvoyants at our desks
trying to divine the message left
in all those little deaths, the dark, childless stars.

A Scrap of Lace

My grandmother used to make Kenmare lace,
      her hook a metal burr
dragging the world slant,
      the chains noosed and trussed,
her patient-handed trickery
      niggling our fates into place.

Like a froth of seafoam or spittle
      it wreathed our handkerchiefs.
Dripped from hems and collars.
      Sat in scalloped rounds
under our blue jardinières,
      perfect and inconceivable as snow.

I used to hate the lace, fuss
      at the prickle and itch,
feel it scratch around my neck
      like a ring of fine-haired
arctic fern, a sheet of lichen
      shot with ghillie brogue holes.

Sometimes I have lifted a piece
      of that lace up to the light
and tried to unwind it with my eye.
      I have never found an opening
in the lashes and loops of it,
      the cobwebbed knots.

But today I read the history
        of John Mathew Cox,
ferried in 1787 to Botany.
        Seven years' hard labour
for thirteen yards of lace.
        I imagine his plain-scrubbed face.

And wonder at the weight
        and heft of those soft boxfuls.
And their usefulness then.
        To pluck a man from his country.
And flog him. And school him
        in justice. And the price of lace.

An Illustrated History of Settlement

Begins with a frame, as if to say here
is the finished, the complete.

Then the last thing on the crosshatched horizon
is a smudge of centuries-dead parrots
in the shining black fruit of cabbage trees.

Above it, a turbulent bluster of cloud.
There was weather. The sky boiled.
And there was water – a choppy wedge
puffed with cutters' sails.

This to introduce the idea of bay,
coastline as opening or entry.

On a far headland, two black men
stand warily, one holding up
a toothpick spear
as if to puncture the clouds' drapery.

Colourless stretch of saltgrass and sand,
middleground as featureless filler.

Closer in, a deckhand unfurls
the rose of a flag in the wind,
and two soldiers squat on a dune,
flintlocks cocked off into the distance,
their heads knotted with tidy black ribbons.

And here in the foreground, a Rubenesque swell
of redcoats tumbling over the beach
like a flock of exotic birds.
Faces fat with apple-cheeked Englishness.
Thighs bulging in white breeches.

And a man in the centre with his arm outstretched –

This is where the eye enters.
And often leaves.

The House on Stilts

Through weaved air, that wedge of darkness
chocked beneath our weatherboard

was no man's land – a fretwork of lattice
checkerboarded the sun, and a fernery

of maidenhair and bird's nest
drifted like sea grapes, tinting light green.

An underground exile, I would cup my ear
up for the thud of clipped heels

knocking like ghosts through the floor.
Now I am the ghost, back down where

the heron-house, the crane-house dips
its white sticks into mud, where black rats

scuffle at night in old fuel cans,
where fishing line frays on copper nails

and film-eyed possums howl and steel their claws.
Born between the wars, between the grey fringe

of scrub and the glass scrawl of reef, this
white ghost-crab tiptoed a century, metal-backed,

and now is history. The gulf yawns – a lifetime
since cyclone rain rattled the venetians

like a handful of thumbtacks, discord
of a continent, but I am there still, midden-deep

in that beetle-black carapace, and the light
flickers in and out like radio static.

Outside, a salt breeze has withered the passionflower:
it hangs dead on the vine. The moon flattens to a crisp.

Hang, we will all hang. Night comes early here –
midges jag in the sky like anxious stars.

Galah's Skull

I find it in a field of feathers, pink-crested,
a knuckle of bone picked clean by the wind,
a pale mohawk mounted on stone.

I bend down. Zeroed out of its head
are two sockets, two airy planets
full of sun, and taking asylum in one

a millipede is coiled, a slick black hypnotist.
Polished, it spirals in on itself
like one of Saint Hilda's fossil snakes

we studied in the school chapel's stained glass.
As if the eye could dig itself into the earth
then extend a curled feeler out, like a fern.

I turn the skull round in my palm like a pebble –
it will not settle. Otherwise, all is still:
the grasses claw in, the world does not tilt.

Even the blue stand of scrub grows over;
it has nothing on its mind. But the skull
will outlast the summer, a thought cut short,

and I will pass it every day as I walk
and stop just here, where the air hones its teeth
on bone, where the mind remembers itself

as a shell, and mourn what was once
a world: one eye rolled to the daylight moon,
the other pressed down into the earth.

Desert Pea

Like the pursuit of fire
a wind stirs the rocks,

summons into heat
a kind of cardinal calm.

This is the violence
of distance.

No end, no horizon.
Only desert floor,

henges of red
and the absolute artifice of sky.

I cannot stand
the certain world:

rock grass and thistle,
animal thirst

invading my eye.
Give me night, the stars

streaming past me
huge and soundless.

Give me the silence
of the mind.

Approaching Paradise

Here in the white, white wing of a gull
you may glimpse paradise. In the flensing sun.
The prodigal sea, bent back on itself,
has the rough green mind of paradise.

Paradise is in the breadfruit's low sling,
the purple scrawl of bougainvillea up a wall.
It is in the yachts' clatter and wheel,
the fishermen's nylon stringing the wind.

You will find paradise in a whiting
drowning in a bucket of freshwater,
in the jammed blade of a fishscale
like quicklime under the thumb.

Women roast themselves in coconut oil
and children run bare-legged in paradise.
Praise them. And praise the black-faced bat
travelling even in sleep through paradise.

This fringe of storm-streaked shacks
with genuflecting surfers riding in,
this line of Norfolk pine. Wet dogs
nosing the muck of a king tide.

Praise the bloated body washed in,
the gentle nibbling of baitfish and bream,
bikini-clad tourists jerked out by rips,
the summer and violence of paradise.

A shark's slit corpse gapes pink on the jetty,
its head yanked on a hook like a sacrifice.
Its shank is smooth and black as paradise.
Men with knives kneel down like seraphim.

II

The Vulture
for Tom Schulz

From his windblown roost, he leans out of himself
into morning, baggy shoulderblades swivelling
in a loose swoop, underbelly bulk
lagging in counterweight to wing,
each stroke ratcheting him into the clear levels of sky.
A reptilian meanness in the face:
raw pink skin rolled on the skull
in slack waves, the whistle flare of nostrils
like a shell's hollows, bubbled tar eye.
By some error, his flawed throat
makes nightmare music: a feline hiss,
the monstrous grunt of sex, all of it hatched
by a mind without pitch.
Brought keeling down to perch
at the swell of rot and bloat
rushing through that tunnelled nose,
he drops foot-first into jungle leaf
and when the jaguar pads away in blood,
stoops to feed. Shaman of transfiguration,
high priest of the day's death march,
he is the afterlife of all things:
child, star, pig, the small circumscribed lives
of the apes and fleas. Attendant, absorbed,
he snips the body from its shadow
with a surgeon's concentration,
sword-swallows tripe rosette,
trotter and gizzard to the hilt,
unzips sun-marinated gristle from skin

with scalpel cut and claw.
His eye flowers darkly.
Self into self without summit,
he gorges in silence, strops his beak,
then hoists out of the corpse on awkward wings,
veering up into the wind's periphery
as if returning from a foreign country,
diving straight into turbulence.

Essay on the Toucan

Osa, Costa Rica

The old colonel keeps his uniform clean:
his kerchief of revolutionary red,
crisp militia black, the absurd cartoon beak.
Proud, dictatorial, he sits out his days
counting in a grubby run-down hole,
he is shunting the dead and the living
into clean blue-lined ledgers,
he is working through the long division
of his shotgun jungle republic
with border and junta, breaking
the shanty towns, corpses, trade winds
into clean fractions, dashing the old maps
with new horizons. He claps his bill,
maniacal, tallies huts and hacked limbs,
the floral-dressed, the modest
severed heads of women,
corrals of them cut down like cane
behind the green screen
of coconut and balsawood,
that leaf-striped territory, he skips ahead,
loses place, starts again, swallowing
each dusty isolate street of cola billboards
and mango stalls in a vast nihilistic surge,
all names addresses faces erased.
All hail our cannibal Caesar,
one bird a nation of the missing
in the macheted ferns and quashed nests,
the dark tribunal of the trees.

The Capuchin

Gran Lago, Nicaragua

I find him down by the boathouses,
a white-haired mystic with canine rhythm.
He paces and paces doggedly
and has a kind of zoo look to his face.
His chain leads down from the soursop tree
to a pat of trodden mud and dung
where he guards a pool of run-off
and stares at his face in the gasoline.
He is a pet of the boatmen
whose blue and green covered craft
ferry tourists to Las Isletas.
I have travelled out there once
and seen his brethren
swinging high in the balsa trees.
Wearing neat black caps and sheepskin
they hung like anvils in the flowers,
ministering to each other
with fingers fine as Julieta cigars.
Like a penitent I approach him
and offer fruit to his terrible intelligence,
a few lime oranges from my bag
dropped into his calabash.
He turns his pink features to the sun
and shuns my offering, curling
his lyre-bird tail around the leash.
Here we are too far from the islands
and there is nothing I can do.
He looks at me with a mendicant air

and dips his paw into coconut cream,
then unhinges a long low howl on needled teeth.
His is the last true religion.
He practises sermons too green to transcribe
on the subject of the Sandinista revolution
to an early choir of sandflies,
then screams like the devil as the boats come in
and packs of gulls on the shoreline
carry on their cheerful scavenging.

The Macaw

Blue is not the colour of paradise.
See the macaw somersault out into a sea

of air, a fork of cracked blue lightning
jagging down the brainless sky,

a rudderless blade. With palette knife
wings, he ekes and scrapes the day's

bottled colour, and lives in air, is air.
Do not call him vacant: he has intent,

though his face is empty, he buffets, a splay
and flash of navy scraps, a brush

of dripping indigo, and stages
a surprise assault on the poor slovenly

trees, the tropic fruit. All entropy,
that knickknack beak. He shakes down

a rain of blood-berries, a rich drench,
and feeds. Chatter is as chatter does:

his ear turns transistor for scratched stone
and rust. Flight calls him, always,

over the oneupmanship of the canopy,
its smug creepers strangling the weak

like fat snakes, that sad hierarchy.
Above it all the macaw blazes, guerilla

sky-mimic flickering along the horizon's nerve,
mad with his blueness, an oceanic

reliquary, deep Cousteau ultramarine
that inverts sky and sea, full bolt blue,

and the sun stings with him. From his view
the Andes are dust, pallid cousins of the Alps,

and the gold-bulbed ants who squall
and clamber in the mud glitter

meaningless as jewels. He fossicks
anxiously through spring's sudden greens,

and each poisonous seed
festers in his gut, heavy as history.

Morning, he sings the bullet out of it,
a dark star dyed almost invisible

against day's amnesiac backdrop.
The seasons repeat. The macaw forgets

nothing; he hoards it all like ambergris.
Palms fray in the wind, fronds drop

ratty showers of budded fringe,
swathes of forest and petty tyrants

shrink. Everything moves into the eye
of the macaw, native and comprehending,

everything sinks into that black bowl.

Life Cycle of the Eel

A flash like silver cufflinks
ribbons off into river grass:
a fluid lick of nickel,
the sidle and slather of eel.
Eyes flat as dishpans
and night-sweat slick,
it flutters out of its den
in slow ouroboros,
a struggling lasso
of almost human skin.
No beauty is quite
like the fan and fluting of glass
it spawns in the reeds,
a clutch of clear jelly streamers
riding the Gulf Stream
to the Sargasso Sea.
Its accent is Scots: elves,
a corruption of eel-fair.
Sexless, according to Aristotle,
born of the slime of sea rocks
or the guts of wet soil.
Today I thought I saw
a silvering eel climb
out of a country stream
and snake its visible heart
through the soaked grass:
migrant of the seas,
line and vector stretching
in a single direction,

its head turned from me
like an omen,
unknowable, knowing.

Orange-bellied Parrot

In the British Museum, its seed-green head
dreams under polished glass
of a long wing-hammering flight south

down through the mosquito net latitudes,
the dark, banana-flanked islands
hunkered in blue archipelagos,

dots of monsoon shacks
on fleeting beaches, cane
plantations streaming wires of smoke,

dropping down, down, further south
to its home country, the grim
scrim of marram and marsh rosemary

marking the boundary of what it knows,
where the turpentine stink
of eucalypts closes in like prison air,

the unending scribbly gums
menace their silver knives,
and the scrawny catstails of casuarinas

whip and whip an uncharted sky.
Its emissary heart wheels out,
sprout-green, staghorn-green,

looking for a familiar *tzeet, tzeet*
in the chipped dialect of corellas,
the chitter of greenfinches,

the cockatoos' and blue-wings' squall,
and, finding nothing but
the roar of parrot talk at dusk

rising hot in its ears, the sour honey
of currants in its throat, it would float
into the leaves like a ghost, green on green,

and from its black coral beak
let its voice inch out on a branch,
a quick orange flare in the thicket.

Green Ant Tarantella

A fiddle of strings:
gold hinges
snap, beads

of Chinese jade
wobble
on loose chain.

Quick sprint
of filament.
Leaf bitumen.

Bows scratch
sticky zags,
batons wave

in grass-green
tack. Morse is ant:
Dash. Dot. Dash.

Three Sketches of a Favourite Cat

I

My moon-clawed killer
masquerades as jungle, mime-still
under the racket of parrots,
prickling in green switch and shade.
He holds his scarred head steady.
Beneath that velvet skullcap
he philosophises in Burmese.
His mind is like a thicket of green bamboo
in which one blue cat is creeping.

II

Sly: his gaze is an executioner's.
Cool as a Cuban sunseeker, he snoozes
in the noonday zoom of flies.
He masks his art in long pink yawns,
kid-glove paws and Zen stretches,
but when a skink
skitters in leaf litter
he is feral, tip-to-toe muscle,
his thoughts still as trapped water,
his tail a bend in the Nile.

III

Sad Caesar, god of the moveable feast,
in the afternoons he presides
over the painted birds' antics
and dreams of the fields at Bubastis:
a thousand cat skulls
wrapped in linen and spice,
cold milk of the afterlife.

Possum

after John Kinsella's 'Goat'

Possum running bristle-bellied through the night
and grunting up the tree. Possum in the early hours
scrabbling in banana mash, moss-nosed
scavenger possum on skinny forepaws
raw pink ears and juiced face,
possum thick with the musk of possum,
possum of the gutturals, umlaut vowel possum,
daylight possum jammed up snoozing fat
in the window well,
night possum revving like a leafcutter on the roof,
bitumen-mouthed growler, rough-throated graveller,
sneakthief scratching the floorboards,
raider possum cloudy-eyed in the fruit bowl,
hammer-hearted nightwalker,
ring-tailed acrobat howling on the whistle sticks,
possum skidding down corrugated iron,
tightrope possum highwiring on powerlines,
possum zapped in a surge
hanging grey-gutted in sun,
roadside possum frozen in car zoom at nightfall,
possum careening on shaky legs
turned roadside possum, possum playing possum
or possibly possum meat, stemmy eye hanging loose
in jelly, tatty-eared, mottled
pelt of possum, bark-backed, burr-furred possum
gunning for a squall, territorial possum
with its claws deep in the side of possum,
possum in perpetual fear

of cat or dog or the quick smear
of possum on the road, passive
or past tense possum, possum on the run.

Muttonbird

They catch the birds and them that have no eggs they let
go again and them that are with Egg they cut the Egg out
of them and then let the poor Bird fly.
          – Lt Ralph Clark, Norfolk Island, 1790

Yes, I have the heart of an oil baroness,
all fish-white and feather-packed,

sweet jellied salt and sullied.
The spring bomb ticks in me,

a slither of gold and whites,
my island child. I hull it swaddlingly

like luck, luck, my heart
piano-wired and plucked

and in the fizz and thresh
of the shoaling sea, in my wild eye

there's a prize for them with knives,
brazen breeches that tramp

the humpbacked beach
bleak as sticks of moon rock

and come taloning
to hook the world from my side.

A Crab Tide

I tread where the mangroves end
in a high tide of red fiddler crabs –
machined pincers, slow primordial heads
like sidestepping stones
wet-cemented in ooze.

From their tatty jaws, new planets
mass and tumble like pearls,
empires of sand moons
forged in the ebb
where barbarians raise their hostile claws.

These coral relics, this foraged rot
are home, or half-home –
we falter, we twostep on the annihilating tide
where each fringe colony
flares and dies, flares and dies,

and breadfruits and mangy palms
thrash as if they might lift off
to seek an older idea of shore,
and beach shacks cling, cling
like limpets armoured in tin.

The idiot Pacific rolls its tongue –
here the razing of culture is ritual,
each anthill perfect and perfectly erasable,
perched where the black backwater
will smash overhead and bury it all.

III

Of Germany

Of a green bicycle with a brown basket
and a slim pack of menthol Vogues
in a Munich café in June, of a black motorcycle,
of riding a black motorcycle in the countryside
to a palace with mirrored rooms
and chandeliers like porcelain anvils,
of Berlin, and the promise of Berlin
on a Monday afternoon, of love
and of Germany, of the scrawny Dalmatian
running free in the Englischer Garten
and the word *Kleine* which is clean as crystal
on the tongue, of your crystalline laugh
and the question of the doubled key,
of blackbirds, of blackbirds carolling
in dark thickets of Bavarian forest
and the Starnbergersee, and the madness
of King Ludwig which also belongs to us,
of folly and of grass, of public squares
and sheets always freshly pressed
before the night train arrives,
of the rough joy of bees whose throats
are tobacco flower and gravel, of south
and north, of winter and summer,
of weathervanes swift as arrows
and starlings oiling the oaks,
of vanity and perishable memory,
of the invisible cats sleeping indoors
and the longest nights, and the beautiful cars
that go so suicidally fast.

Late Hammershøi

after Vilhelm Hammershøi's Interior with Woman at Piano,
Strandgade 30 *(1901)*

The world won't come in, not tonight.
The door is open, the window is closed,
the linen stiff and white as an owl's wing.
Saucers stand sentry over the table.
Butter has gone soft in a dish.
And what the black-haired girl slumped over
the piano plays is forever hidden,
her arpeggios deliberate and slow as the sun.
Hammershøi loved the light. Light streaming
like a woman's hair through the window,
light wetting the mouths of wineglasses,
light slanting its long towers on the floor
like the travelling teeth of a comb.
Particles swimming there in light's archery.
Hammershøi's friends worried
this obsessiveness was symptomatic:
the long hours alone, his cool privacies.
To love light above all, whose main habit
is dissolving. The critics tired of it.
Study after study of Ida's back,
years spent leaving or entering a room.
Light is routine, they said.
But that was his genius: light survives us.
In its long wandering, in its patient
illumination of hallways and doorframes,
of streets and alleys in our absence.
And now it is evening. Hold your breath.

The room is quiet, a chair is empty,
doors open on doors, the piano is darkly gleaming.
Velvet creeps over the hammers of the keys.
The world won't come in, not tonight.
Only cascading notes float like dust
in the air, soft as ash. Mozart, it must be.

Collioure/Love Poem

An open window
on the Mediterranean.
Mid-afternoon.

Yachts
leaning
in salmoned light.

A green sail
leafing
into distance.

Salt breeze
deliberating
what to do next.

And the luxury
of turning
back to the room.

Beauty is a Ticket of Admission to All Spectacles

Even those you do not want to enter –
Goya's picador strutting bold as a macaw
in tasselled blue, and the bull on docile knees
in the straw, sinking into slaughter.
Klimt's Judith, her lips softening as if for a kiss,
her arm arcing into the minute
when she unstems the fruit of a man's head.
A swan's neck muscling
like an anaconda up Leda's ruddy thigh
or the plumed pageantry of a Dutch hunt,
hooked corpses of spatchcock and duck
contorted like gymnasts in a Delft kitchen.
Knobby lemons tumbling over wood,
the sun a filigree on all that feather.
These things are easy to enter. I remember
my father shooting a crow one Easter,
the muzzle of his air rifle
against the paling fence like a stick of black slate.
How the crow's breast gleamed
as he wrapped it in a sheet of newsprint,
the tyranny of its open eye,
as wild and dark as anything.

In the Mauerpark

No sadness, my friend, no sadness.
Under the lindens, in the time of starlings,
the pinwheel on your balcony spins
like a summer dress, so fast, so fast,
the women you knew sleep like stone,
old metals burn under centuries of grass.
No time for sadness, no time.
Turkish boys play soccer in the Hermannplatz,
a public clock ticks where we stand,
the passing subway shakes the ground.
It is summer, no sadness, we are free,
your parents will live, and call you in,
your broken glasses will return to you.
Our hands will touch in another time.
The starlings are dark in darker leaves,
a terrible fluency, *Liebe*, *Liebe*.
At the Reichstag tourists weep in their coffees
and a graffitied *why* on a city wall
drifts like an airship, to where, to where –

Primavera: The Graces

We know when the wind bends down
to tangle the raw silk and the oranges
thicken their perfume that our natures
are dark after all. No time for angels now.
It is spring. Death is in the trees,
in the petals shining underfoot like glass.
Let the dance quicken in the blood,
let it shake the speared buds down
like hail, let it hollow the minds of men
and bring them to us, howling like dogs.
See, we move through the black wood
like gods through time, turning and turning
as if it is all reversible: the light sieving
through the branches, wet grass
arching up to our touch, the pale seeds
and their red and white unpeeling.
The end is in the beginning, it is our song.
The men will come, rough mouths agape
at the crabbing of light and shadow
at our feet – we have no stake in it.
Our art is too long; the circle
will not break. Only the birds hurtling
like flung stones know the truth:
it is in the tiny fandango
of their pulse, in the leaves scratching
them through the air, in their descent
which is short and unspectacular
and spills out of them like wine.
Fear it: your lives are short too.

Poem for My Father at Sanssouci

Vineyards tumble downhill, nobody knows where.
The rain comes and goes, it is impossible to rely on.
Quiet garden paths of snapdragon and hedge
lead to a weeping tree; its branches sweep the ground.
An eagle's stone eye stares over the water
and the slow herd of clouds turns north to Berlin.
Life is not yet over. The red rococo silk
still curls with fleurs-de-lis, putti cling
to the ceiling and don't remember why.
A terrible purity moves in the high leaves.
It's worse that way, to live for centuries.
Better to wipe the long rooms of childhood clean,
grey hours in Harrogate, buried bottles of whisky.
One by one they fly out like sandwich papers
into the blue sky, the grey sky, small suicides.
No one will lead you, no one will follow
when you migrate to darker eaves.
I have seen the swallows foraging there
for winter material in the meagre fibres.
They gather twigs and drop their feathers.
That is their sadness, they ask for nothing.
Death will find them in the high towers
where they wait in makeshift nests:
the wind will seal their eyes together
so they forget even the light, and shut it out.

The Quattrocento as a Waltz

So long to the madonnas stiff as hairpins
and their blue capes like bells,
to the angels with Grecian cheekbones
and fishscale wings,
so long to our downturned faces
and halos bricking our heads with gold.
The inquisition of the light is over.
It was false, the teeth of an old woman in a jar.
It was unsteady, pouring in from everywhere.
It ruled our canvases like a sad autocrat
with its endless directives and its long, long gaze.
Here's a baby: he's an apparition.
Here's a god: he's a shank of meat.
Too celestial, too cruel.
Let the darkness shake out its bolt of silk.
Let it roam over us like a blind tongue.
Let it bury its razorblades in the citrons
and its hooks in the wild pheasants.
Open the window: outside is Italy.
A fat woman is arguing over artichokes,
someone is dying in a muddy corner,
there's a violin groaning in the street.

Interbellum

after Edward Hopper's Summer Evening *(1947)*

Late April: forsythia
        grafts to green wood,
napalms into blossom –

simple yellow in the yard, earnest,
        pliant as youth.
Inside, buttered rooms

are cooling. There is no
        reason to leave
this crate of light,

no new world to step into –
        the difficult prairie
grass is blacked out,

the windows tarred:
        nothing is not hidden,
night limes everything.

Listen: each minute subtracts
        a cricket's voice
from the wind

then another enters, flares
        like a cigarette
to take its place – you could not

call it song, this unison,
        it is without end,
it circles the way

cotton moths dogfight
        to the death, to claim
their ration of light.

Rain, Ravello

In a small yellow room above Amalfi
I am learning blindness from the rain
which redrafts itself sheet after sheet
and is finally like and unlike nothing but other rain.
Rain slanting in a slow cramped hand, rain failing
or falling emphatically, rain in quick chromatics,
rain in light-fingered counterpoint to the murderous spring.
Everything that can be lost is lost.
Somewhere in the lemon trees, a mourning dove
sings privately. Art is not enough, not nearly
enough, in a world not magnified by love.

Embouchure

Funnel and funeral lily,
my father's trumpet
nestles in blue velvet,

an oiled ear
of steamwhistle metal.
Sunflower-brassy,

it arranges its cornucopia of air
in still-life pall:
a horn of plenty utterly empty,

mute and boldly bald.
The mouthpiece gropes
in perpetual O –

no breath to moo out
a yellow lone post
or blast a rattatat retort

like knuckles on doorknob.
Embouchure, the word is –
you hold the neck

with a death-grip and force
lips in hard kiss against it.
Tulip-tall, my father used to pace

our hall's slate
playing boiled Brubeck jazz,
penny-bright as a showgirl's tassel.

Now he cannot raise
the breath and instead
bends underwater

vowels from it – whales calving –
then strands the golden knot
in the instrument case.

He will not hold his face still enough;
he will not hold his face.

Aubade

for Bronwyn Lea

White light over Rome today –
gulls drift mindlessly towards the Vatican,
their wings watery blue as the cirrus.

Today I want to watch and not to be,
to let all this shift as thought
shifts, as the gulls' grey feathers sift

in slants and dream diagonals, as the eye
enters the windowpane and finds
the poplars alert like dark hares' ears

in blocks of citrine terrace,
the flat wintry street, and beyond that
only the weak film of morning,

lobotomised calm, delicate
and thin as rain, born of nothing
but the pale itinerant air

from which everything begs
and which itself asks nothing.

Against Ingres

And the women?
　　　　— Théophile Gautier, *Constantinople*

She is looking over her shoulder still,
her back patient as polished maple,
a line the colour of buttered toast
unfurling down her spine in an arabesque
to her tailbone and buttocks,
which are long and slumberous as a mare's.
Nobody knows how she moves
the mysterious knot
of her body, her shoulders hunched
like a cormorant's, the taut triangle of black
tucked in her elbow's crook
and her one weakling foot that drifts
boneless. Cold blue silk on the skin,
a shadow curling under her right breast.
Her masters are long dead. The women
she oiled faithfully every morning
are distant as the cries of a peacock
in the sultan's garden. Even fat, lazy Nilüfer
who scratched graffiti into the walls
and swore as she brought in the figs
is centuries away, talking sulkily
to an overseer with a thin white beard.
Here there is nothing – this room,
this bed, the crumpled linen pinkish
as if it has absorbed the colour of her flesh,
the gold fly-whisk and her gaze

which is disinterested as salt
and could be saying anything –
I'm tired, I'm cold, I'm hungry.
Ingres, it's late, it's raining, the servants
and girls are dreaming in bed
of knives and birds that cry like wolves
and by now even you must know
what it means when a woman turns
her back on you.

Liebesträume

After he leaves, she sits at the piano
and thinks that even if this is the way the thing ends
she should have still played him the Liszt,
and she studies her hands. Held like this
they could almost belong in a Vermeer,
each finger a fact in the clear Delft light:
the small room rinsed with shadow,
red apples by the window, and everything
dazzled by what does not appear.

Umbrian Sketch

Orvieto

As the afternoon stretches out
the duomo's too-tall black and white spire
drags like a needle in the clouds,
flocking children chase their shadows
to the cliff's edge, crying like gulls,
and the pale madonna in her golden chair
austerely contemplates the façade of days:
the colossal, classical pain.

Reclining Nude

after Lucian Freud's Benefits Supervisor Sleeping *(1995)*

So we reach the end of our argument with beauty –
the pink nude sails like a conch out of her girlhood,
exiled from its whorled walls and tiger shell,
a refugee in her soft new body.
It happens swiftly, while she sleeps – one day she is monstrous.
She loafs like a cloud that has drifted indoors
and no longer knows what to do with itself.
In his studio, drop cloths slather the windows like lard,
apricot roses fray, olive upholstery fattens
into the great abstraction of her body –
flesh squidged over the couch in a thick salve,
hillocks trowelled with creamy putty.
She has outlived sex. As she poses she dreams
of long walks down Job Centre's fluorescent halls,
the monotony of standing-room queues. Her eyes roll in sleep
the way a bar of light rolls under photocopier glass,
smooth as charity. The artist tells her to crawl, spread
her legs, grind her arse like a pig.
In the scrunched paint rag of her face
there is a crease, as if to say here intelligence lives,
here the rational, the sceptical, but also
something that rebels, says *you are rump, hog, beast.*
He swaddles her hips and boulderstone breasts, grouts
her moon-drum stomach in blue oil,
winnows a hog's hair brush down her caesarean scar.
She has kernelled another body in her body there,
perhaps one of his, it doesn't matter, he can't
remember if he has had her, the point is

she understands largesse, he can see from the way
she dangles the hock of her arm casually
as he paints between her legs –
there is nothing to which she will not submit
like a nihilist Cimabue madonna
who lifts the son of god on one hip
but shrugs her other shoulder
as if to dismiss the weight of her gift.

Goya's Dog

after Francisco José de Goya y Lucientes's The Dog *(1820–23)*

Who among us saw the dog that day,
who could have said
whether it was holding its head
above the surface
or going under?

The Flowers on His Bedside Speak of Eternity

And are swiftly cleared by an axe-faced nurse:
peonies, soft pink explosions in the bin.

Petals rondelle from a single stem. When speaking
of ash, we say *sift*. Time, you used to be

such a stable thing, but you clip-clop,
you hobble in this dim white ward. His face

slackens, turns. Yet it is I who wobbles,
who will topple first. The peony's root

is cut before its pompom flowering,
the neck slipped so quick in water

the head cannot detect the break.
Like easing into bathwater, his death.

I will go first, when he forgets. But who
will stay sitting beside his bed, and whose

face does she wear, the one who looks
so like someone's daughter, or the woman

who used to bring – what was it? – milk,
or the marzipan in? He is calm. It is not

material. Listen, I tell you: it is lonely
to scrape eyeless among the stars,

eyeless and faceless. Oblivion creeps in on a tray.
He never liked flowers. Take them away.

No End to Images

No end to tissues of tears beside the bed
or to avenues of trees and cathedrals,
no end to bee-eaters in the rose apples
or summer on the balcony in Neukölln,
no end to the pharmaceutical clouds over Kraków.
No end to the hour I stood and shook
like a leaf in the shower's privacy,
no end to my name, snagged like a burr,
no end to the body which is colossally small
with its pains and plainer longings.
No end to grief, never any end to that.
No end to the silver train stalled in Budapest
where I wept in the empty sleeper,
no end to iron shoes along the Danube,
to history, the convalescent light
that falls on my desk so evenly,
no end to the gardens of Europe
with their murderous symmetry,
no end to picnics on the forest's edge
or piazzas of pure Carrara marble,
to cruelty, madness, oblivion,
massacres and women's scarves,
the hunger of wolves, ripening stonefruit,
no end to fear and secret police,
and no end to Bach fugues on the turntable
whose ideas resolve so cleanly
into a life infinitely more gentle and orderly
than our fraught morning fights
or the cries we send echoing at night
down the hollow halls of love.

IV

Insurgency

How perfect the past is.
Everything happens there once.
Snow geese hunker
on the frozen lake.
Cotton moths tremble
in the dark.
Wild watermelons swarm
with seeds.
And the errors
we have made
we have made completely.
Like the fire-blue
pit of glacial ice
called terminal moraine,
things assume the hardest shape.
But still, this insurgency.
The door unanswered.
The stone unthrown.
The captive
on the other side
who waits and waits.

Night Sonnet

Speak softly now: the neighbours are sleeping.
Cars drowse under the window quiet as mousetraps,
smoke winds up silently from an ashtray
like the plumes of a deep-sea squid,
a grit of light trembles on our white bedsheets.
Who are you beside me, irresolute
as a flag in the wind, your face gliding
into wolfish dreams, your breath dragging
like a styrofoam cup in the street?
I like watching you like this, running
bodiless through the alleys of a foreign city,
hunted by the sound of a stranger's coat.
The stone tilts – spears of blue shadow.
The stairs are steep, there is nowhere to go.

Impressions of April

Yes, that was when. Your unforgivable visit.
Like a film set, my fifth-floor apartment.
A skylight, a sketch, a square of dull sun.
You sent tulips. They stood tall in a jar.
A call to somewhere far away, very far:
Australia. Apologies in the dogwood
and the days arranged like other flowers,
white starbursts bent on stalks.
It's futile to make much more
of mothers on the Hudson's bank,
overwrought fire escapes, neighbourhood teens
folding in that shabby laundromat.
I unpacked. Scarlatti was the only news.
Waterlilies swam blue at the Met. I went
but only for the Pacific canoes.

Morningside Spring

California oranges and painted plates,
the paperback psychology of days
dog-eared with dependencies:

the telephone wintered in its nest,
purple crocuses in violent waves,
the air-raid howl of the trees.

Across the street, a new tenancy
in the bricked-off estate:
two kids unloading their lives from a van.

They stand in the drab brown beds
of the communal garden,
him smoking, her nursing a glass,

too exhausted to be angry,
though her face is small and set
and in the blunt slump of his shoulder

against the fence there is the force
of a branch that could break, a weight
nearly not borne, though the bud

clings greening on its cold perch,
each hour more pointless than the next,
the minor horror of a blue mattress

on sidewalk display, the trophies boxed
and taped, the resentment shared,
the closed parenthesis of the gate.

Mercado

Just you and me on the balcony,
eating papaya with plantains and coffee
and bread rolls and tea
and boiled eggs and coffee
in these wrought heart-backed chairs,
looking down on the market square
at the watermeloned stalls, all pink and green
and the fountain's clam-shell scalloping
where boys lob rocks in shallow yellow
and wade in the water deep, deep.
It's a simple affair:
no need to complicate things.
Just talk to me of Pergolesi and the Italians
and the way the Roman summer is –
I know the way the summer is –
then take me to the plaza for a drink
where a flurry of fabric flowers
more peacocked and flocked
than a hat of Carmen Miranda's
winds up a pole to the Latin flag,
and beyond that white kite sticks
like crosses are stamped in the distance.

Garden Apartment, Taube

Beautiful Schumann on the speakers, beautiful platonic
Clara Schumann behind the scenes, doyenne,
muse of the late quartets, sleeping perhaps with Brahms,
all that madness and grief. How quickly we are lost
in these petty names – you and I, he and she.
Now we try to find the German word for it
in a tangle of leaves, in his garden apartment
above the Spree. And you, that old you
to whom I used to speak, you will be married,
you will become a stranger to me,
a little sunlight, a little Turkish wine in a glass,
ceramic doves on the sill of your street.
The Algerian. Her killing smile. Will she last?
The impasto of trees annihilates so greenly, so fast.

Via dell'Amore

Nothing will destroy the Ligurian Sea
or that sheltered spot where we sat
by Riomaggiore's corrugated rocks
and ate a loaf and Spanish salami
with some local plonk whose stubborn cork
you knifed on the winter quay
as the rain drove down in acrimony.
Love, love, like a faded song –
I remember rain, the vigilant stare
of a pregnant black cat
whose belly swung with wasted heat.
Was that the end of love?
No money, in no month to swim,
we stayed until failure hit the rock.
The sun did not come back for us.

The Atlantic

Bombed on Old Fashioneds at three, at four,
you snore beside me like a bull
cocooned in puritanical grey flannel.
I twitch out the early hours to the methodical clip
of your heirloom watch,
my face buckled to your wrist,
a flaw in Burberry glass.
Beside the bed, your peacoat and pocket square
slump, limp as evidence:
we will wound each other yet.
Old friend, you were right when you said
this can't go on. Still, I find your all-American jaw
in the dark and thumb its edge. It drags
against my palm like a panther's tongue,
no balm for the blade. The weekday
shaving lotion you slather
skulks behind the bathroom mirror,
creamy as money. My mind strands
on the rocks of your cropped New England vowels,
your cock-of-the-walk brag about the brood
you plan to raise, the faint praise
you gave when you said I was a perfect cocktail date:
the kind of girl smart enough to just let *talk*.
Now you lord it in a blue-blood job
that will make you a millionaire by forty …
If only I could wait. Yesterday's *Times* said
more body parts washed in at Oak Beach:
Long Island Sound's serial killer
stalks his hunting grounds while we sleep.

Nobody knows who he is or where he lives
but we are safe here from his atrophied love.
Last week a jogger found a pair of hands
tumbling in the sand, dumb as tongues.
The sweat strangles. I feel your breath at my neck,
roll to the cold side of the bed.
Two hands. Last summer we swam
so far out in the Atlantic we struck a rip
and scissored our legs in the salt
as Montauk went a blue darker than ink.
Now you pinion my shoulder like an anchor
and knead me from deep in your dream.
Something will have us in the end.

O California

I want to wake in the lagoon of the sky
where sunlight binds the mutilated palm-tree dawn
like duct tape, an aerial shot rolling and rolling
out of town in the muffled trunk of a brown panel van
along the death roads, the desert roads, the hairpin
turns, California, the desert silvering in my eye
like a coyote, I want to swim in the jewel-jade pool
of your lonesome foothill vowels,
stretch out under the mirroring clouds
like a million rooftop deckchairs, feel
that blankness unfurl in my mind like luxury,
California, your beautiful blankness, your sheen.
O, shake me a basil gimlet at Silver Lake
and tell me about your tattoos, *hermana*, how death
is that bad tooth wobbling in my head,
in my head, California, that skyline that breaks
into backdrop hills I know like nostalgia, pink saguaro
and sumac, the ripe berries smashed like bodies,
each ragged cactus cross hoisting up against a silver
desert screen, California, and night that goes on like a
      drive-in,
palms exploding like napalm, fireworking over everything.
I want to ride the long smooth tan body
of California, I want to eat the bear of the flag
of California, I want to roll like a corpse off the highway
of your chase scenes, I want my perfect teeth
preserved, California, my teeth buried
in the earth like a curse, California, and won't you show me
where the bodies are kept, California,
won't you show me, show me, show me.

The Invention of Ether

Flayed of colour, February's premature stars
gasp in iron over Boston Common
where the thoroughbred brick houses stand.
In the Public Garden, green flakes
over the pilgrim graves,
and Lowell's old Civil War monument
hurls its jagged shadow like a lance.
Now a dignified pair of hounds
breaks from their handler's leash.
I see them circle in the yellow willows,
gums peeled back in stillborn smiles,
on the hunt. Murderously young …
Down by Frog Pond mud bulges with spawn,
black comets flicker in slime. Life surges on.
And the Japanese redwood whose leaves
rust the ground each fall
still guards the ether memorial,
that turbaned doctor
who blots out the world in marble
as his patient's thighs tremble and sag.
Pain! Like a hammer to the knee
it jerks in and out of focus, always throbbing.
'Can't they see I'm heartbreaking?' –
wasn't it Cal who said that, sobbing?
Remember last year? You flew out East
burbling with an infected chest,
and, agonised, proposed in the park.
I refused, then nursed you back
after your shivering break.

Still, I cling to the sting
like the slobbering octopus
I failed to rescue
from boyish torturers
on a Sicilian beach:
hopelessly suctioned, unable to release.

Last Goodbyes in Havana

Midday cracks like a cool blue cup.
We drink a last rum among the tanned couples
and kiss pre-revolutionary glass to our lips,
smooth and honest and scratchless.
Beneath us, waves smash the Malecón
with a force that could break our lives.
Your eyes are hidden behind your sunglasses.
Your hand shakes. Now and then you turn a page
of *The Dangerous Summer* and sigh
accusingly. We have cheated, certainly. Lied.
Days we have fought float over us effortless
as grease. Soon I will take a night flight to the Pacific
but there are no reasons left to be sorry.
In Manhattan a woman is waiting for you
whom you have taught more than enough
about patience and her possible life.
You tap your knife against your plate
and turn a page. Down the cliff, Cuban boys
are diving off the stonewall into distance.
Their young dark bodies gleam with promise.
They kick down, then rise from the water like seals.

Postcard from Another Life

A green pine bench above the giant thresh of the Tasman.
And a herd of dusky Merinos whose fleece
was mottled to the same heather as fieldgrass.
Huge heads of stone making a valley in that place.
How we sat there feeling the unreasonable
heat blowtorch our cheeks. Greek olives,
then the cold white wine. Unwilling to admit
such pleasure could exist. Frightened, too,
by its corollary. So awake from talking all week
and not being done talking. Being the only
ones to make the pink rock, swimming all
the way out in that arctic water. Bleached sun
on quartz, and us wanting to believe this
was our ordained life. But the unimagined
still happens. Later that day the whole valley
was razed by wildfire. We took the highway so far
over the limit it was hard to make the hairpins, ash
massing in front and behind. No surprise he left
and his love with him. Still, when I remember
it ranks with the great pleasures. Late Rossini.
Lemon granita in Taormina, that abiding
sourness on the tongue. A high tide stealing
across the Piazza San Marco, and fattened gulls
lifting from the reflections of café chairs.
Local men have to pull on rubber dungarees
to wade home in the evening there. You could hear
them cursing, but also now and then laughing.
All Troys are sacked sometimes.

Ensign

Your parcel of French Romantics arrived today –
late cellos and violins, the end of an epoch.
Fact: the mind is outstripped by wood and catgut.
Fauré with a frayed moustache on rue de Madrid,
going deaf, scribbling desperate quartets.
Magnard, burned alive by the Germans in Oise.
We have so little time left. We should love.

The Hazards

How calm, how sudden the strait was that day –
humpbacked rocks sloping down into the sea
like the end of a long argument,
everything now peaceful again, but tiptoeing,
and past the sweep of gravelly beach
huge pink ledges lopped off in the water like bread-ends,
here and there a stump – call them islands – breaching at
    elbow angles,
and the slumbering bergs underneath, snub-nosed as marble.
At our feet, digger birds with shiv faces
cracked limpets solemnly for meat, blacksmithing,
and further out, specks of seabirds fishing the whitecaps,
then that awful calm clear green all the way to the Antarctic.
Everything tasted of the sea, was of the sea.
You thrashed out first, hard, with your varsity calves
towards a far granite cheek,
the tiger's stretch of your body
powerful but ungainly, your torso turning
from side to side like something the ocean was rejecting,
and in a wild kick, a leaping up,
I saw you as a stranger might see you then,
your head straining above the surface
like a diligent retriever's, your eyes fixed ahead
as though the future were an island
you needed to reach without me,
and I knew I would never unlearn love like this, as distance:
your mild Midwestern college cut
dark and unstable on the horizon,
your too-white boxer's shoulders finite and ungiving

as you climbed the scrambling side –
you who would live if I died, *you* who were not I –
and I felt the shock, the parry
of my heart's start and stop: my life, my life.

Notes

The book takes its epigraph from the second movement of Brahms's *Ein deutsches Requiem*, which in turn takes its text from the German Luther Bible, 1 Peter 1:24: 'For all flesh is as grass, and all the glory of man as the flower of grass. The grass withereth, and the flower thereof falleth away.'

'Medusa': *medusa* is Italian for jellyfish.

'The House on Stilts' was written after reading David Malouf's fourth Boyer Lecture, 'Monuments to Time', about the experience of living in a Queenslander house.

Several poems in this collection are ekphrastic. 'An Illustrated History of Settlement' responds to a number of paintings depicting first colonial contact in Australia, chief among them Emanuel Phillips Fox's *The Landing of Captain Cook at Botany Bay, 1770* (1902). 'Collioure/ Love Poem' responds to Henri Matisse's *Open Window, Collioure* (1905). 'Primavera: The Graces' takes as its subject the three graces in Sandro Botticelli's painting commonly known as *Primavera*, or *Allegory of Spring* (1482). 'Against Ingres' responds to Jean-Auguste-Dominique Ingres's *Grande Odalisque* (1814).

'Beauty is a Ticket of Admission to All Spectacles' takes its title from a passage in Ralph Waldo Emerson's *Journals and Miscellaneous Notebooks* (5:414): 'Beauty is a ticket of admission to all spectacles, to all hospitality.'

'The Invention of Ether' refers to the Ether Monument in the Public Garden of Boston Common, which commemorates the invention of the use of ether as an anaesthetic and bears the engraving, 'To commemorate that the inhaling of ether causes insensibility to pain.' Robert Lowell, known to his friends as Cal, once said to Helen Vendler, 'Why don't [the critics] say what I want them to say – that I'm heartbreaking?'

'Last Goodbyes in Havana' responds loosely to Raymond Carver's poem 'Morning, Thinking of Empire'.

Acknowledgements

Poems in this collection have previously appeared in *The New Yorker*, *Poetry*, *Slate*, *Agenda*, *Michigan Quarterly Review*, *The Cincinnati Review*, *The Massachusetts Review*, *Antipodes*, *Stonecutter*, *Australian Book Review*, *Australian Poetry Journal*, *The Weekend Australian*, *HEAT*, *Cordite Poetry Review*, *Blast*, *Canberra Times*, *antiTHESIS*, *Higher Arc*, *The Stinging Fly*, *Ooteoote*, *La Otra*, *The Best Australian Poems 2010*, *2011*, *2012*, *2013* and *2014* (Black Inc.), *Thirty Australian Poets* (UQP), *Young Poets: An Australian Anthology* (John Leonard Press), *Australian Love Poetry 2013* (Inkerman & Blunt), *Prime: An Artist's Folio* (Otago University Press), and *The turnrow Anthology of Contemporary Australian Poetry* (Desperation Press/turnrow Books). Many thanks to the editors of these publications.

I thank Sharon Olds and Bronwyn Lea for their generous and thoughtful readings of this book in manuscript, and Charles Simić, Meghan O'Rourke, Yusef Komunyakaa, Matthew Rohrer and my friends at NYU, especially Jeannie Vanasco, for their comments on individual poems. I am also grateful to my editor, Felicity Plunkett; my publisher, Madonna Duffy; and the team at UQP for their expertise and enthusiasm. This book was completed with the assistance of an Australia Council Literature Residency at the BR Whiting Studio, Rome; a MacDowell Fellowship; a Marten Bequest Travelling Scholarship; and a Fulbright Scholarship – my sincerest thanks to those institutions for their support.

Also by Sarah Holland-Batt
ARIA

Winner of the 2009 FAW Anne Elder Award
Winner of the 2009 artsACT Judith Wright Prize
Winner of the 2007 Thomas Shapcott Poetry Prize

From this living tinder
I have made
a thin blue flame.
It will not stay
unless I cup
my palm around it.

Sarah Holland-Batt's *Aria*, winner of the 2007 Thomas Shapcott
Poetry Prize, is a striking debut. Like piano music heard through a
high window, the language is haunting but entirely of this world.
The poems are awake to the dark constellations of art and history,
to what momentarily is, and to what flows endlessly on.

'*Aria* is one of the most accomplished first volumes I have read
in a long time and Holland-Batt is a poet worth taking special
note of.' *The Australian*

'Holland-Batt is gifted with an acute ear. For a poet in her mid-
20s, much craft has been absorbed.' *Canberra Times*

'*Aria* is a joy to read. Holland-Batt appears to be a major poet
from the start.' *The Age*

'*Aria* is a most haunting and impressive debut volume.'
The Sydney Morning Herald

ISBN 978 0 7022 3675 4

David Malouf
EARTH HOUR

Winner of the 2014 Queensland Literary Awards –
Judith Wright Calanthe Award

We sit in the warm dark watching
container-ships ride
on blue-black moonlit glitters.

After long
journeying arrived at the high tide
of silence, after talk.

David Malouf's new collection comes to rest at the perfect, still moment of 'silence, after talk' following its exploration of memory, imagination and mortality.

With elegance and wit, these poems move from profound depths to whimsy and playfulness. As Malouf interweaves light and dark, levity and gravity, he offers a vision of life on 'this patch/ of earth and its green things', charting the resilience of beauty amidst stubborn human grace.

'*Earth Hour* is a beautiful, spacious volume that will repay re-reading not simply because it is – with a characteristic Maloufian lightness of touch – preoccupied, every so often, with last things, but because it shows, as his prose always does, how good an ear he has as a writer.' *The Sydney Morning Herald – Spectrum*

Earth Hour 'contains some of the most charming poems you will ever read.' *The Courier-Mail*

Earth Hour 'brims with the intelligence, elegance and wit we have come to expect from Malouf. I could go on, but I will leave you to discover the pleasures of this volume for yourself.' Stephen Romei, *Weekend Australian*

ISBN 978 0 7022 5013 2

UQP

Kathryn Lomer
NIGHT WRITING

A vivid new collection of poetry from the winner of the 2008
NSW Premier's Literary Award – Kenneth Slessor Prize for Poetry

We've already lost a lot
and want to make the most of what is left.
The whole epidermis is already dead;
the rest will follow suit:
now is the best place
for everything.

With sensual, fresh and graceful energies, Kathryn Lomer's *Night
Writing* is a collection that moves between the grounded and the
whimsical. Each small gesture has expansive implications; each
poem is jewelled with reflections and woven with slivers of insight
and bright fragments of mirth.

'Hungry curiosity and the tussle between rational and intuitive
knowing are hallmarks of Kathryn Lomer's poetry. As in earlier
books, the poems in *Night Writing* both embody and dissect
their themes – the nature of love, or language, or light, for
example – with verve and lexical richness. Lomer's poems are
full of phrases that you want to carry away on the tip of your
tongue. This book might, like one of its poems, have been called
"Dear Life" for it embraces life emphatically.' Sarah Day

ISBN 978 0 7022 5003 3

UQP